THE HONEYCOMB

NANCY BOTKIN

POEMS

stb

STEEL TOE BOOKS

est. 2003

THE HONEYCOMB

Also by Nancy Botkin

The Next Infinity

Bent Elbow and Distance

In Waves

Parts That Were Once Whole

TABLE OF CONTENTS

For my sister, Linda

"Freud once said that of all human obsessions, the strongest is a desire to habitually rely on memory, when the truth is that memory is full of holes. We fill those holes with ghosts."

— Lee Kravetz

A PATH TO A CURE

They're going fast, those pristine figurines,
those white angels. The curve of a wing is a revelation.
Who wouldn't want a cherub sitting on a smooth rock
or wedged in the dirt? Those colorful windmills
that mesmerize as they spin will be a nice distraction
as the dog days approach, days without rain, days
when sprinkling the lawn seems like an exercise
in futility. Let's face facts: you won't be 20,000 feet
in the air anytime soon unless you're the risk-taking
type or loaded with antibodies, so the solid earth
is here for you in ways that you've taken for granted.
You must embrace opportunities since embracing others
is frowned upon. But, back to statues, which are tumbling
in many cities. You've heard Christopher Columbus
bit the dust, dust being what we're made of
and what swirls about the cosmos, but no one
puts Christopher Columbus between the impatiens
and the daylilies anyway. It's nice to know that the sky
is there and that things grow underneath it. I'm working
on the hypothesis that silence and marble and breath
thundered together call up the low notes. You cannot
tell me that wind sweeping over the grass is just wind
and not a symphony, not art darkening the world.

MAKE-BELIEVE

What I saw in a winter sky was not
the angelic order, but a tattered
handkerchief stretched above the playground.

When I opened the hymnal, the notes
were shaped like lemons, and what I heard
in the voices was silence, the aftermath
of a house blown open,
empty.

One year I knew beating wings, and in another
snapping bones.

What I took for guilt was just my hair
wet against the back of my neck
and anger was a gate unlatched and frozen.

Make-believe was like the tide washing up
with its scalloped edges, white like a cloud,
fluttering like a butterfly.

OH, THOSE LIPS

Screw four-leaf clovers. We had red wax lips
sold in the candy aisle for a penny. We batted
our eyelashes, cooled ourselves with makeshift

newspaper fans, mugged for some invisible stranger
with a wide-angle lens. We rose from our flat
selves, crystallized like sugar on a string to capture

the starring role and live like the girls across
the highway who spun in the direction of the earth's
orbit. Our mother laughed. She knew about longing,

cigarette smoke curling around her head, hair twisted
around prickly rollers, a little beer for shine, her
housewife-self transforming into Marilyn Monroe

or Jackie Kennedy. We all looked up when we heard
the roar, slick Mustang gunning up the street, racing
toward a sunset so blood-red we could taste it.

POEM ENDING WITH WARHOL

If everyone jumped off a bridge,
my mother asked with an edge of anger,
would you jump too?
But I thought of the girl I most admired
and we were so golden
walking along the trestle.
She says *I'll go first*
and I say *Let's go together.*
Holding hands, we leap, a high-
pitched whistling in our ears, our
hearts bottled in our throats.

Two bodies in free-fall, the river
rushing toward us with flittering
hands, cushioning us
for a future, after all.

You're dreaming, my mother said,
waving away some harebrained scheme of mine
which sent me back
to the mine—to the mind—my golden labor.

Andy had bad skin and a skeletal frame
and famously said we should fall in love
with our eyes closed.
He was always thrumming,
a bee boring
the honeycomb
again
and again.

that education is miraculous
I was pinned behind a desk
only to look at pictures
ethereal clouds
for which I was
here on earth
on a paper map
memorized their capitols
of a pale blue mitten
eyes ahead
shaking her ruler
blowing one long steady
and everyone else's
lowered her arm and the
but Jesus had better things
music was a great respite
tables and capitols
golden light leaked
to create shadows
ones apples throw
perpetual rounding
day and night and I couldn't
between light and dark
in massive halls at the sight
flames held high in praise
to step out of the dry ice

day after day
nailed to the floor
of floating angels
the great afterlife
instructed to strive
we located the states
irregular shapes
Lansing, Michigan in the middle
the classroom was a great theater
teacher in front
or raising her pitch pipe
note which to my ear
was useless once she
song was underway
to do than sweeten our voices
from multiplication
at the end of the day
from under the blinds
beneath the desks like the
in still lifes
of night and day
get enough of the play
which led to my heart swelling
of thousands of quivering
while I waited for David Bowie
and take me home

JUST FLY

Crows you are *caw caw caw*ing today jogging my memory

gathering on the lawn for a cabal confrontation coffee klatch

dotting the landscape like the kids from the old neighborhood

Catholic families every house had four five or six kids always

foraging relentlessly complaining stuck out our tongues to catch

snowflakes danced twirled chased each other down the street what

do you want to be when you grow up the nuns were grooming us

to be nuns or mothers I see you walk with real authority swagger

I wanted to be an angel without having to die just fly as I did

in dreams low above the trees looking down on the neighborhood

kids running across white snow white as my mother's pills resting

in a wheel a game of roulette or a clock keeping the hours of each

day until it adds up to nothing but quick shallow breaths the rise

and fall of a chest oh you've flown now left in a rush but you'll

be back soon calling all around these dim gray-shadowed places

A MATTER OF TIME

For a while she got lost, or she glazed over, or she
was struck like a gong at the mention of The Depression.

Edith held court on high school, the one dress, the one
pair of stockings she rinsed out every night, and her own

mother's sadness that desperate night they had bread
sprinkled with sugar for dinner. First she wore giant

wrap-around sunglasses, and then a giant wristwatch,
its face the size of a pie tin because she was going blind.

I winced when she described the office visit, the nurse
prepping her for an eye injection with only a couple

of numbing drops. We're doomed to not really see
because we haven't been there, but I was there the morning

she died, the sun barely up, and touched her cold, stiff
hand, but that's not really knowing death or the something

that is there and the something that is not, like those ethereal
floaters that appeared when I was young, after I set up

the plastic toy oven that housed a hot bright bulb
at its center. It made the cake, but the light threw spots

into my field of vision for a minute or two after I got
close and inspected the workings, but never inspect

the workings of ovens, or wall outlets, or wristwatches,
especially wristwatches because you will learn something

about time that you can't undo even if you walked
backwards toward the sunset and into yesterday.

SUNDAY MORNING WITH ELM

we were cutting some of the branches off
    the elm in the front yard

how long—20 years   Kelsey a teen
when it was a foot high

the debris piled up around us

we started cleaning up
          lopping the branches to fit into

the waste bin the morning thrumming with its

      morning noises a bird's golden bell

our friend Tim gone 2 weeks now

      just suddenly gone

took a break and introduced ourselves

to the new neighbor
    Katie
          and her daughter Charlotte

wispy blonde hair
starting kindergarten in the fall

the former owner Jo lived in the house for 51 years

a riot of tulips arrived every spring
      I love spring said Charlotte

          the yard impeccably kept

the morning Jo left she sat down on the driveway

      86-year-old woman on the hot concrete
her head in her hands
weeping wept

      my whole life I imagine she said to her daughter
crouched beside her
      Jo widowed four years

our elm smaller now

      letting more light through

INDIANA STILL LIFE WITH MELLENCAMP

Old Glory flapping in the foreground, and the place
in collapse just the way I like it. Rotted wood,

mossy wood, leaning barns, and plenty of chinks
to let in light,

slanted just right.

Barking dogs on the loose, looping
a muddy path. Sweaty brows and back porch

beer. Over there

is a young John Mellencamp sporting
cool-guy shades, and a cigarette dangling
from his lips.

He scans the sky for rain, or inspiration—a worm
hole to slither through and emerge bigger.

Three children on a dirt mound
opening their arms to creation.

It's all art.

We're tenacious like the sprawling cornfields
that survive the seasons, and its song is endless.

We've logged plenty of hours
in the *crow sun truck rust rain* rhythm.

It's wind gusts, guitar licks, and *It was an accident!*

Yes, John,
it's a jubilee,

the eye following blood and blossom,
landing on
just the right kind of lonesome.

ICELANDIC

I'm down on my knees
scraping paint off

the floor with my thumbnail,
washing my hands
over and over, but it's like trying

to get *blunt force trauma*
and *strangulation* out of the news.

I went back and forth between *Icelandic*
and *Moonmist*,
colors suggesting cool and distant,
colors with blue

undertones. I peer through the vertical slats
at a slab of November sky, dark and bruised,

but what a lovely idea the leaves have of
striking gold,
catching fire,
flaring red.

It makes
cleaning them up less of a chore,
but what do you do with a body?
What to do with a baby

who cries and cries?

Here's one idea: take her
to the thigh-high weeds
and bury her under an ivory moon,
always so indifferent to bare arms
and the nape of a neck.

One by one, I held square samples
against the wall
which produced a false reading

like a faint pulse
or the moon behind clouds,

and what does a baby girl do in the afterlife?

Here's one dream:
the dirt takes her apart, takes away
every color that made her human,
but she undoes the gray buttons, the brown
blood fades, and she floats into a room
that holds its champagne promise,

unaffected by morning
light or evening light,
or lamplight,
or candlelight.

Or time.

I'm grounded here for days,
the paint hardening on the brush,

and I hold a swath of sky in my mind,
the pink one, reminding me

of feverish skin, blush,

cooing, and silent laughter.

FROZEN

Even in the places that invite
   calm, I fail. So, with my
head face down
   in the cradle, I stare
at the floor, but mostly
   my eyes are closed
while I listen to the music,
   the quasi-soundtrack
similar to what I've heard
   in the airport tunnel
but with lapping waves
   and seagulls' cries,
and I try to imagine
   I'm on that beach sitting
on the sand, toes buried,
   because, after all, it is warm
here under the sheet. But
   the impeachment hearings
are getting underway
   this very afternoon, so
it's hard to be "in the moment"
   as they say. It's hard
not to think about my
   daughter's job interviews,
my students' failure to revise,
   or the cold snap that's
gripping the mid-west
   in the middle of November.
Mr. Magic Hands tells me
   he hates winter right before
I hear the click of the cap
   on the bottle of oil
and before I feel the pressure
   of his thumbs as he slides
them down my spine,

and before he digs them
into my neck where it hurts
from all the squats and overhead
presses and deadlifts
I've committed to because
I'm trying to undo osteoporosis.
When it's time to turn over,
I lament that I'm not eating
enough kale. I'm not
eating *any* if you want to
know the truth. I'm not
eating cottage cheese either.
What I really want
is an experience like Madonna's
in her "Frozen" video,
the part where she falls
backwards in slow motion
before she hits the parched,
cracked earth and breaks
into dozens of black birds
that fly up and away. Oh,
to fall and break and then soar
skyward, a being transformed,
flapping a dark wing in the
foreground, the whole
scene washed in a palette
of blue-gray, all of it
composed and beautifully
conceived. Stillness is one
thing and transformation another.
He takes an index finger
and makes a circle over
my heart and says,
To the source of all that is,
and that gets me thinking
about origins and flight
and flesh and skies
and poetry while I dress

and prepare to enter
    the daylight, my thoughts
bouncing, not quiet
    and still.

MACULAR WRINKLE

You tip your head back
to receive the drops

in the semi-darkness of the ophthalmologist's office.

You blink and wait.

With your head pressed against the plate
            and your chin in the rest,
the doctor says, *look at my ear,* and touches his left lobe.

The light is brutal
            as it skates across your glassy eye
making a 180-degree sweep.

You shield your eyes as you step into daylight
as if leaving a movie theater. You try

to turn off the drama while finding
            your footing among what gleams—chrome
fenders, foil wrappers and aluminum cans.

Some days you want to push
            the plate away and get up
from the table of the body.

A generous reading says the sun wants
to console you, but the light is brutal.

You cast your eyes downward onto a puddle

that's communing with the sky,
            eager to be its medicine cabinet mirror
swinging on its hinges,

tempting you to come closer and look inside.

17

STATE OF GRACE

For taking the wings off bees, for holding a magnifying
        glass to the ants, for those transgressions
the remedy was communion, that wafer, that flat

unleavened bread, which to receive you needed to be
        in a state of grace, without sin, but who were they
kidding? In the confessional I was helpless, ticking off

a list of sins less exotic than the insect torture variety so
        I could get it over with and do my penance, recite
the requisite Hail Marys and Our Fathers. Back home

I ordered up Kool-Aid. Top shelf, I said in the mother tongue,
        which got them laughing, the adults who were
never without sin as far as I could tell. They were not pure,

or pure of heart, or young at heart, as Frank Sinatra
        recommended. *Fairy tales can come true*, he crooned
through my father's stereo speakers while they swilled

booze, lied, and told dirty jokes. Their pumpkins would never
        be carriages, only misshapen pumpkins, discolored
and pimpled. They were people—no magic, no wings, no prayers.

ROE V. WADE

You just learned that women are on the cusp of losing
control of their bodies so you roll down the car window
and breathe what you think is pure air and look at the sky
which appears to be blue and admit to yourself you don't
know anything for sure which is why you'll go home
and tie a string to a tin can and take it into the yard at night
and sit on the cool grass where you'll whisper back
and forth with your best star who makes up her mind every
single second to send her light to you from a place so far
away you can't stop crying from the wisdom of it.

YOU'RE FLYING WITH MIRACLE

The young Latino in the middle
seat wears a giant rosary
around his neck, and as we taxi
down the runway, and after
the flight attendant shows us
how to buckle in, secure
the oxygen mask, and inflate
the life jacket, he makes
the sign of the cross
before kissing the body of Jesus.
I figure I'm covered.
Also, Miracle, the seagull
on the wing flap,
is in my line of sight.
Airborne, the boy looks
at his phone, slim girls
parading in skimpy suits
by a pool, some raucous
movie. Up here, things
are strange and I could fall
in love with death
not by violent impact,
but by plunging
through a membrane
of cold thin air mingled
with cloud
fluff, like birth
or youth, all that
roaring,
unaware if
or when
or how
I'll land.

#FREEBRITNEY

Surely the airport is an essential symbol
        of the American Dream. Arrival
and departure, departure and arrival

are in the history of its people. Although
        those who arrive and depart
also wait. Hundreds of weary passengers snake

through the maze set up at O'Hare for the unenviable
        stamping of the passport
by sullen, serious men who never smile, who, Houdini-

like, suck all the energy from the room. In a not-so-subtle
        act of defiance, I kick my carry-on
bag forward. There's nowhere to go: we shuffle,

we shift our weight, children press
        their foreheads to the nylon crowd
control belt. A father bends to his daughter and says,

"You aren't the only one not having a good time,"
        but what time is she supposed
to have, this firefly trapped in a glass bottle? We

can all hold our breath, turn blue, but we'll die
        before we're free, and not a fountain
in sight to toss a coin, a grand disappointment after

arriving from Spain, land of fountains, land
        of open-air cafés, land of cobblestone
streets and *duende*, for Christ sakes. The officer

patrolling the line is not happy either, bearing the burden
        of the crowd's anger. We need to feel
human. Our arms are folded and completely useless,

unless we're swiping the phone endlessly. We can
           all root for breathing, but it's
elusive. At this point we're ready to break so, yes,

free Britney and whoever is being held against
           her will. Perhaps
someone has pulled up Britney on a phone,

viewing her on a GIF, her head tilted, lips
           parted. America's seductress
arrives, and she keeps arriving.

THE WHITE ALBUM

Oh, to fall backwards
and stare into a milky sky! My arms
and legs moved as if someone were
pulling a string between my legs,
and if I could stand it, I'd rest my
bare fingers on top of the snow. It
was like touching the Pope's sleeve
as he granted me absolution, my spine
light as a feather and alert to the shape
of ghosts. It's pointless to think about
a snowman's inner life, but I imagine
its thoughts are circular, rolling bands
of white, reminding me of a gymnast
somersaulting and handspringing across
the mat in a leotard, sparkles twisted
into her hair reflecting the camera
lights, a blinding brightness
like the sun at dusk hitting
a storefront window where they
are having a two-for-one sale
on silk sheets. Oh, to fall
backwards into bed, arms
spread like a Posturepedic
Christ and stare at the paper
boats sailing across the ceiling,
lying very very still,
sticking the landing.

SONNET FOR THE STILL

I bet you can't keep a straight face for one minute, we used to

challenge. *You. Can't. Laugh.* Or go without blinking, a favorite game

of who-can-go-the-longest, which, back then, I foolishly tried to do

with a mannequin when I wandered away from my mother in Hudson's

Department Store, before finding my way to a three-way mirror, covering

up my good eye so the lazy one would snap into place. Even then

I knew it mattered how you looked, but who would paint their face

silver and be a stone-still statue in the hot sun like you see in New Orleans

with the hope that the touristy-types will toss a few coins in your hat?

Still, I think stillness is admirable and sometimes not a matter of choice,

like cattails in the wind, or when a doctor enters the examining room clutching

your chart and says, *I'm sorry.* Everything comes to a stop when your eyes

meet. You strive for balance, unlike the flickering fluorescents above you

behind the white ceiling panels, but chances are you will falter.

POEM ENDING WITH MAGRITTE

Wearing a mask has always been controversial.

Often said: She seemed sincere, but I don't know . . .
Overheard: There's a persona, and then there's a *persona*.

When I was getting an oil change,
the TV was blaring in the waiting room,
a stupid station selling its own brand
of truth and democracy.

"Yes, I concur," said the woman next to me with her eyes,
since we can't recognize each other's faces.

To undo the elastic straps from behind our ears
is to be vulnerable.

Witnessed: She marked him and then wiped
the lipstick off with her thumb.

Mouth to mouth is *hard.*

A mask *and* sunglasses?

Maybe we should go by *feel*, the way the blind do.

In *The Lovers II*, the two figures are kissing,
each one veiled to the throat, heads like fists.

What it takes to survive, maybe.
Poor Magritte.

THE BLACK CROWS

Petals on a black bough? How about
puffed-up crows on the white snow?

No ideas but in bling! Such as the sun
scaring up little diamonds sitting pretty

atop, and very little depends upon them,
really, even though they're beside the black

crows pecking like angry chickens before
the arrival of unseasonable rain followed

by a freeze which precedes a crowd of people
talking endlessly about the white glaze.

TIME SENSITIVE

Here it is: the heart weighs, roughly, eleven ounces.
        Which is why on a calm summer night,
alone with the stars, you can't hear it beat, even
                when you tip your chin toward your chest,
just as the earth tilts when making a slight
                adjustment at the solstice. You're more likely
to feel a pulsing in your ears. When people have
                told me that their lives were imploding,
their stories have to do with the heart—the failed
                marriage, the foreclosure, the forensic
evidence—their faces closing down like dying
                flowers. I kick the dust off my shoes
here in Indiana, what we call the heartland, one
                of the center states that seems essential
to the country's survival. There's something sturdy
                in our pipes and valves that's critical
to the health of Selma and Sacramento. Yet,
                if you say you're from Indiana they wonder
what you're doing living among the cows
                and the endless ribbons of road. I read
that a plane had to turn around and go back
                to the airport to retrieve a human heart,
precious cargo that didn't transfer, the recipient
                waiting in another state. Now we're
getting to the heart of the matter, we say in anger,
                when the cold nugget of truth is sitting
there exposed, and today it was the hospital
                personnel in their white jackets,
shifting their feet, blood rushing in their ears,
                as the plane glided onto the tarmac.
You can't undo the problem of the body,
                but you can put a heart in a container,
carry it by its handle, and walk as fast as you can
                to a person whose chest has been cracked
open without skipping a beat. Few will ever hold

a human heart, but no one can look
at the cosmos without one, or a dilapidated barn
        in a blue-air sunset, or a fallow cornfield
covered with frost. For a minute on that cold
        table, the patient had no heart at all. True
or false? We are heartsick when we are without.

THE GUN VICTIM'S MOTHER IN RUINS OUTSIDE THE COURTROOM

The cracked glass of her, lightning splitting the tree of her, her heart carried away by flood waters, rage banging its cymbals, the smell of kerosene, the mob torching the city of her, her grief expanding in a cup of tears, the beaten rug of her, the cut engine of her, the hollow skull swinging from the key chain of her, the wolf of her howling at the full moon, her body a country she's running from, her mind a vast field with one lone crow, a milk-blue silence beneath a midnight snowfall, a needle touching down on her pristine black vinyl, her soulful song endlessly spinning.

SELF-PORTRAIT AS A MARK ROTHKO PAINTING

What good is piling shame
on top of lofty dreams?
The world is divided in twos,
maybe threes. I, myself, have
been preoccupied by three
blues in slightly varying
shades. I'll take smoke
along with raging fire.
I've walked a thin black

line between passion and
smoldering indifference.
I've learned that cranberry
juice and bourbon don't mix.
Sometimes it's a question
of what's on top—manic
energy or deep dark regret?
Some days those heirloom
tomatoes sit right on top
of the dirt. I'm a creature
of habit hoisting block
upon block. I'm calm.
I'm lucky. I'm out for
primal blood. I dream

my life into symmetry.
No point in changing
shapes now or closing
the gap between solemn
light and pinkish dark.
I'm guilty of making sharp
divides with no gray
areas. I love the horizontal
line where burning sky
meets fertile earth.

I would like to know
the pleasure and the pain
of crossing that border.

HOUSEWORK

At the time I chose to keep it to myself. At the top of the narrow
stairway in the attic room I succumb to darkness hunched like
an animal, to the dangers under the bed. Down two flights, in
the depths of the home, my mother bent at the ironing board tipping
the water bottle, dabbing the yellow cap, sprinkling the shirts
and then rolling them like dough. There was a clean smell of bleach
rising from the scalded cotton. I was learning to fit the shoulder tightly
around the narrow end of the board. I had to be quick. I had to be deft.
I wanted to guide the steel tip with precision. I wanted to twist
my body, wring out the fear I was wearing so I could be lighter.
I wanted to float like the soft ding of a dinner bell, so I checked
the closet and under the bed where dust lurked and a man with a knife.
Each night I looked up at the crucifix and then pulled the covers over
my back while my mother was combing a familiar dark, putting the white
shirts on hangers, buttoning the top buttons, hanging them in a neat row
in the laundry room, sleeves puffed with air. Soon, and once again,
my father's arms and shoulders. The phone ringing like an alarm.
"No, just housework," she says. The long cord in a tight coil, a lifeline
or shackle or home plate. Always the endless shirts, hissing ghosts.

NEGATIVE CAPABILITY

A crystal flute has heft, which is why people covet

    the champagne when viewing abstract art

at a gallery opening, not because they're thirsty

    but because they need something to hold—

and to hold them in place—when facing the unknown,

    heads tilting this way and that. There's always

one annoying person who says out the side of their mouth,

    "It doesn't make sense," or "Jesus, I could do *that*."

I'll tell you what's not easy. Showing your father something

    after he's dead, which is what my grandson suggested

I do with the rocks we collected. He was anxious to show his

    father the speckled pebbles jiggling in his pocket and

assumed I would do the same. I told him my father was

    dead, that both my parents were dead. After a

pause, he said, "They'll be alright." His words hung

    there quietly, not bothered by tricks of the wind,

or by the amorphous shapes landing on our shoulders, or by

meaning trying to touch us with its busy, irritable hands.

WATER

The splash pad
is the new swimming pool.

Water erupts, shoots a foamy froth
that sends kids shrieking

with glee. If I listened
to everything the rain said, it would

encourage my bluest blue.
This bubbling is unbearable lightness.

Being that I am a student
of the heat, I can gush with the best

of them. I praise the smack
of the sun, the slap and gurgle that nests

in the womb of June. I wrap a towel
around Calvin who thirsts for nothing.

A stuck heart can be jarred loose by water.
It's the world's greatest idea,

and right here, right now, it's renewing
its own life. It's inexhaustible.

POEM ENDING WITH O'KEEFFE

You speed across the blue water
to an island where horses wearing blinders
clip clop along muddy streets.

You bicycle to the steps of The Grand Hotel,
and your mind's eye opens
to polished marble and smooth mahogany.

But, the flowers! In front of you, lively
cancan kickers. A chorus line of brilliant,
ghostly, ravaged, burning things.

Can you see what O'Keeffe saw in a whorl,
in a dark center, how red
becomes something other than red?

What do you do with a flower and a blank
canvas? You enlarge the flower.
You magic the real.

NOTES & ACKNOWLEDGEMENTS

The book's epigraph is from Lee Kravetz's *The Last Confessions of Sylvia P: A Novel*, Harper Collins Publishers, 2022.

p. 12: "Icelandic" was a semi-finalist for the Jeff Marks Memorial Poetry Prize sponsored by *december*. In remembrance of 11-month-old Mercedes Lain whose body was found in a shallow grave in Starke Co. Indiana in 2021.

I would like to thank the following journals in which these poems first appeared:

Poetry East: "Water"

Gyroscope Review: "A Path to a Cure," "The White Album," "Make-Believe," "Oh, Those Lips"

Third Coast: "#FreeBritney"

Sleet: "Time Sensitive"

december: "Icelandic"

Indianapolis Review: "It's Clear to Me Now"

Nancy Botkin is the author of *The Next Infinity* (Broadstone Books, 2019). She is the judge of the annual chapbook contest sponsored by Wolfson Press at Indiana University South Bend where she taught writing for many years. Now retired, she writes, makes collage art, and refinishes furniture in South Bend.

The Honeycomb by Nancy Botkin
Steel Toe Books Chapbook Award

"Magic the real" writes Nancy Botkin in *The Honeycomb*. These poems explore the necessity of art and the imagination, the ability to see that even the darkest places can resonate with beauty when the eye is trained to see it. Memory, that constant companion, also resonates; its fuzzy and fickle nature can be buoyed by artistry. As she combs the past, she discovers that a rich inner life is a powerful defense against a random and precarious existence. She delivers this message with clear language, subjecting the ordinary events of life to pressure, making them new, bright.

PRAISE

"At its core, *The Honeycomb* is a book about flying. Sometimes high, sometimes low, and often on the wings of angels. The opening poem sets the stage, telling us, 'The curve of a wing is a revelation.' Revelations build throughout. Women and the travails of modern life soar like birds, connecting us with both the celestial and the everyday. Botkin finds solace in the works of artists like Rothko. 'I love the horizontal/line where burning sky/meets fertile earth.' And I loved the duality of these poems, the attention to winged things that invite us to investigate the many phases of existence through a wider lens."
–Constance Brewer, Editor, *Gyroscope Review* Poetry Magazine

"In *The Honeycomb*, Botkin explores the borderland between tragedy and comedy, taking us to the edge of life's gaping emptiness and its bewildering fullness. In richly imagistic poems characterized by frank vulnerability, she shows us how to live with contradictions. This is an achievement of the spirit."
–Joseph Chaney, Director of Wolfson Press

stb
STEEL TOE BOOKS
est. 2003

Steel Toe Books
steeltoebooks.com
Poetry
The Honeycomb
Nancy Botkin

$13.00
ISBN 978-1-949540-44-4
51300>

9 781949 540444

This Time This Place

Susan Suntree